Tim Furniss

OUTER SPACE

Illustrated by Gordon C. Davies

PUFFIN BOOKS

Words in **bold** type are explained
in the glossary on p.30.

Contents

The Solar System

Did you know that millions of people live on a **planet** in outer space? This planet is called Earth. Earth travels around, or **orbits**, a star called the Sun. Light from the Sun takes eight minutes to reach the Earth. There are eight other planets that orbit our Sun. The furthest planet from the Sun is called Pluto. Light from the Sun takes over five hours to reach Pluto. The nine planets and the Sun are called the **Solar System.**

Pluto

Neptune

Uranus

Saturn

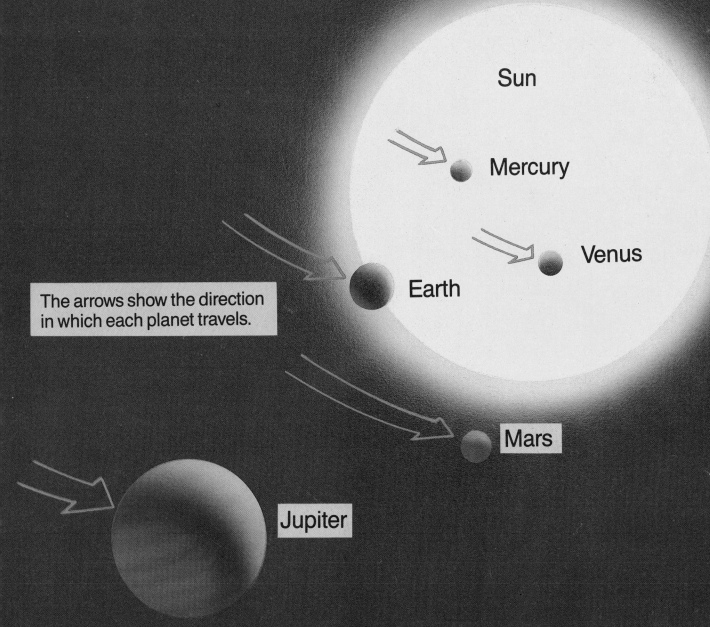

Sun

Mercury

Venus

Earth

The arrows show the direction
in which each planet travels.

Mars

Jupiter

Sun

6

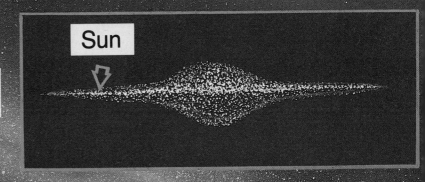

Sun

This sideways view of the galaxy shows its disc shape.

The Milky Way

Our Sun is just one of billions of stars. They are spinning around in a shape like a disc. The disc is called a **galaxy**. If you go out on a clear night you can see hundreds of stars in the galaxy. You might also see a fuzzy trail in the sky – that is called the **Milky Way**.

The Milky Way is the centre of our galaxy and it contains billions of stars. Light from the Sun takes thousands of years to cross from one side of the galaxy to the other.

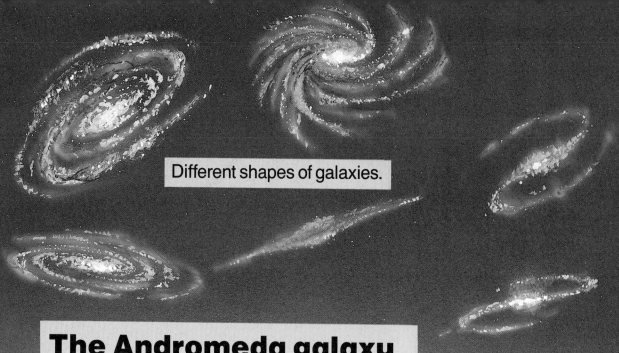

Different shapes of galaxies.

The Andromeda galaxy

There is not just one galaxy. There are millions of other galaxies in the **universe**. There is another galaxy quite close to us called **Andromeda.** It is a fuzzy patch in the night sky. What you really see is the light that comes from Andromeda. The light took two million years to get here.

The Andromeda galaxy.

NGC 7331 is a galaxy like our own.

NGC 7331

Looking at stars

For thousands of years people have tried to find out more about stars. The light from a star is called **radiation**.

Stars also send out radiation we cannot see that travels through space as radio signals. **Astronomers** use special telescopes, called radio telescopes, that can pick up these signals. Astronomers have learned a lot about the universe using telescopes.

In 1957, Russia launched the first spaceship and since then, spaceships have helped us find out more about outer space.

Astronomers look through a telescope to see the radiation from a star a long way off.

Giant radio telescopes.

11

Jupiter

12

Pioneer 10

How big is space?

Distances in space are so enormous that it would take the fastest spaceship over 100 million years to reach the nearest star. Light travels very fast but the light from the nearest star takes more than four years to reach the Earth.

In 1972, a spaceship called **Pioneer 10** was launched to explore the giant planet Jupiter. It took *Pioneer 10* thirteen years to travel to just outside the solar system.

Jupiter is a beautiful planet.

The first spaceship

Space exploration began in 1957.
Russia launched a spaceship, called
Sputnik 1, into orbit around the
Earth. It was a **satellite** that sent
back "bleep, bleep" signals to Earth.

The rocket that launched
Sputnik.

Sputnik

Earth

After three months _Sputnik_ fell out of orbit, pulled back to Earth by **gravity**. It was travelling very fast from space and when it hit Earth's **atmosphere**, this caused **friction**. This made _Sputnik_ so hot that in the end it burnt up.

The first man in space

Four years later, in 1961, Russia launched the first man into space. His name was **Yuri Gagarin**, and he became a hero all over the world. His spaceship was called *Vostok*. *Vostok* had a **heat shield** so that it did not burn up during **re-entry** into Earth's atmosphere. As *Vostok* came down to Earth, Gagarin jumped out. He landed safely by parachute.

Yuri Gagarin inside *Vostok*.

Later, other Russians and Americans flew into space. Finally there was a plan to land men on the Moon called 'Project **Apollo**.'

Vostok during re-entry.

Gagarin parachuting back to Earth.

Landing on the Moon

In 1969, America launched the spaceship *Apollo 11*. *Apollo 11* flew to the Moon. It took *Apollo 11* three days to get to the Moon. There were three men, or **astronauts**, on board. *Apollo 11* went into orbit around the Moon. Two of the astronauts landed on the Moon. Their names were **Neil Armstrong** and **Buzz Aldrin**. Neil Armstrong was the first man to walk on the Moon.

   He said, 'That's one small step for man, one giant leap for mankind.' Altogether there have been six Moon-landing missions and twelve men have actually walked on the Moon.

Apollo 11 lifts off for the Moon.

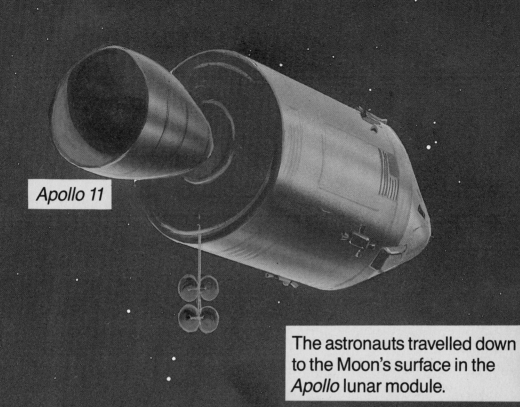

Apollo 11

The astronauts travelled down to the Moon's surface in the *Apollo* lunar module.

The first men on the Moon.

The space record holder

Most spacemen fly in their spaceships in orbit around the Earth. Some have lived and worked on **space stations**. One Russian space crew flew in space for 236 days, which is nearly a year. The commander of this mission was **Leonid Kizim**. He has flown in space three times. His total time in space adds up to longer than a year and so far he holds the space record. He was the first commander of a space station, called *Mir*. Russia plans to fly more crews to *Mir*, who will stay there for over a year.

Space station *Mir* in orbit above Earth.

The shuttle is a working spacecraft. A damaged satellite can be repaired in space.

The space shuttle

The American **space shuttle** was the first spaceship that could be reused. The commander of the first space shuttle was **John Young**. He has flown into space six times and has walked on the Moon. In 1986, a space shuttle called *Challenger* exploded. Seven astronauts were killed. This stopped space shuttle flights while scientists tried to find out why the accident happened.

The space shuttle coming into land like an aircraft.

A space station

The space shuttle will be used to help build a large space station. There will be laboratories on the space station where scientists will carry out many experiments. They will try to make medicines and many other things in the **weightlessness**. They will observe the Earth and the stars. It will even be possible to repair spaceships there. Spaceships will be launched from it. The space station will be a base.

Future space stations might look like this.

The first space stations will probably be like this one.

Learning about the planets

Many spaceships have explored the planets without astronauts on board. Instead they had special equipment and cameras that sent back pictures and information to Earth. In this way, scientists learned a lot about the planets.

Mariner flying above the planet Mercury.

A *Viking* capsule parachuting down from the main craft to land on Mars.

An American spacecraft called *Mariner*, took pictures of the planet Mercury and found it looked like the Moon. Russian spacecraft landed on Venus, where it is hot enough to melt metal, and sent back colour pictures of the planet to Earth. *Viking* spacecraft landed on Mars and studied the red soil there. Spacecraft called *Pioneer* and *Voyager* took pictures of the beautiful giant planets Jupiter, Saturn and Uranus.

A *Viking* space probe taking samples of Martian soil.

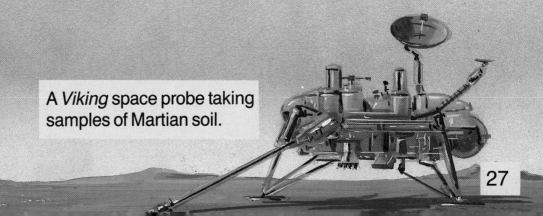

Using outer space

Space exploration has really only just started, but we are already using space. Satellites are used to relay telephone calls and TV pictures around the world. Often on sports programmes people say, 'relayed straight to you by satellite'.

Different kinds of satellites.

Some satellites look at the weather on Earth and help the scientists to tell us what kind of weather to expect. Other satellites observe the Earth. They help **geologists** (scientists who study what the Earth is made of) find oil and minerals. They help map makers too.

Ships and aircraft find their way using satellites. So, you can see that space is becoming a very useful place.

Glossary

Andromeda   A galaxy near to ours.

Apollo   The name of the spaceships that took men to the Moon.

Armstrong, Neil   The first man on the Moon.

Astronomer   A person who studies the universe.

Astronaut   A person trained for travel in space.

Atmosphere   The gases around a planet.

Friction   This is caused when one object rubs against another, making heat.

Gagarin, Yuri   The first man in space.

Galaxy   A mass of stars together in space.

Geologists   Scientists who study what the Earth is made of.

Gravity   The force that holds everything on to the Earth.

Heat shield   A special coating or barrier that stops a spacecraft burning up on **re-entry.**

Kizim, Leonid   The man who has spent longest in space.

Milky Way   The name of our galaxy.

Orbit   The path of a planet travelling around a sun, or of a satellite going around the Earth, Moon or another planet.

Pioneer 10   The first spacecraft to leave the solar system.

Planet   A world orbiting around a sun.

Radiation   The light, or other signal, a star gives out.

Re-entry   When a spacecraft travels back into the Earth's atmosphere from space, where there is no atmosphere.

Satellite   A spacecraft which

orbits the Earth, sending back information or relaying TV programmes or telephone calls around the world.

Solar system   Planets going around a sun.

Space shuttle   A spacecraft that can be used again.

Space station   A huge spacecraft in orbit around the Earth, where astronauts and scientists can live and work.

Sputnik 1   The first man-made Earth satellite.

Sun   A star.

Telescope   An instrument which, when you look through it at the sky, makes far away stars and planets appear closer and easier to see.

Universe   Outer space and all there is in it.

Weightlessness   Where objects float around because there is no gravity to hold them.

Young, John   Commander of the first space shuttle and the only person to have made six flights into space.

Books to read

Ardley, Neil *Just Look At The Universe* (Macdonald, 1986)
Furniss, Tim *Space* (Franklin Watts, 1985)
Lawhead, Steve *Howard Had a Spaceship* (Lion, 1986)
Mason, John *Space Travel* (Macmillan Education 1986)
Parker, Steve *Space* (Step into Science series Granada, 1985)
Rickard, Graham *Spacecraft* (Wayland, 1986)

Index